Electric Dress

Poems

Joanne Diaz

Barrow Street Press
New York City

Cover Image: Atsuko Tanaka, *Work (Hoops)*
(1975-00-0301-000)
Courtesy of Museum of Contemporary Art Tokyo
Tokyo, Japan

Cover Design: Catherine Charbonneau
Interior Design: Michelle Caraccia

Published 2026 by Barrow Street, Inc., New York City
(501) (c) (3) corporation. All contributions are tax deductible.
Distributed by:
Barrow Street Books
c/o University of Rhode Island
English Department, Swan 114
60 Upper College Road
Kingston, RI 02881

Barrow Street Books are distributed by Itasca Books Distribution & Fulfillment, 210 Edge Place, Minneapolis, MN 55418, itascabooks.com. Telephone (844) 488-4477; amazon.com; Ingram Periodicals Inc., 1240 Heil Quaker Blvd, PO Box 7000, La Vergne, TN 37086 (615) 213-3574; and Armadillo & Co., 7310 S. La Cienega Blvd, Inglewood, CA 90302, (310) 693-6061.

Special thanks to the University of Rhode Island English Department and especially the PhD Program in English, 60 Upper College Road, Swan 114, Kingston, RI 02881, (401) 874-5931, which provides valuable in-kind support, including graduate and undergraduate interns.

First Edition

Library of Congress Control Number: 2026930816
ISBN: 978-1-962131-12-4

CONTENTS

III.

I.

Invocation to Electricity

You who are free
from the burdens
of animal, vegetable,

and mineral states,
you who are perverse
in your transit

through all three:
what use is it
to speak your name? You

are ubiquitous and constant,
more faithful
than any human, you

who bound my parents
in a helix of wires
and sound and light,

two ordinary people
charged to maintain
your circuits all their lives.

Today, at the supermarket,
I saw you in the bolts
of lightning that rose

along the arms
of a man's sweatshirt.
When he turned

I saw the letters—I.B.E.W.—
sprayed across his chest,
and the fuse that connects

all workers—thousands,
for decades—the electricians,
the telephone operators,

the welders,
the lighting technicians,
wizards whose wires

weave through me.
In this state, I see
every piece of amber vibrate,

a vestige of when you
were mere spirit
or twitch, pure radiance

beyond the harness
of any human.
Always your eros stirs

the universe; you
are a catalog of the crimes
done in your name,

some of which
are archived in a trail
of inert paper,

bleached by the machines
that feed from you.
You thrive in every melody

we transmit,
in familiar voices
that shuttles across

the nation, in every flash
of light that glows
until each wire

is the dust that speckles
our galaxy, and only you
can truly reanimate the dead.

Illuminated

Yesterday, for the first time: a flicker.

The light was a brass circle, bright as day—

no glare, no matches, no nauseous smell,

the shape of a dropping tear.

Inside, fire; inside, pearl.

A man could sit down and write for hours

without the consciousness
of carbon.

Illuminated, this could go on forever:

the premise

of progress.

Photograph of Thomas Edison in Mathew Brady's Studio, 1878

If you look quickly,
        the phonograph—

its long cylinder,
        its metallic gleam—

might look like a rifle,
        but no: this is Edison's

newest baby, capable
        of talking, laughing,

singing, whistling.
        Edison has arrived

at Brady's studio
        with his new suit,

his pose, his certainty,
        this invention, and Brady,

the most famous photographer
        in the world, the man

whose glass plates froze
        the Civil War,

is descending
        toward his nadir.

When the soldiers
        who fought came back,

they had no desire
    to see the glass plates

that carried
    the horrors, no desire

to sit, genteel now
    and in civilian clothes,

for the man
    who created them.

Sometimes everything
    quickly dismembers us,

and it's the re-membering
    that's hard, and slow,

not just for the soldiers
    who made it back alive,

but for this photographer
    made infamous by war,

now bankrupt, his mind
    a bench used to the habit

of breaking. Edison knew
    that Brady was destitute,

so he promised not to sit
    for any other photographer.

Even so, eventually,
    when the streetcar

careened down the avenue,
        that grinding of steel

was a siren song
        and Brady ran for it.

Nickerson Beach

Today, August and Joe dodge
and dip with the tide that pulls

toward the Rockaways in one direction
and Jones Beach in the other.

As the Atlantic Ocean rolls
slate-gray and vast and brilliant

in the sun's white light, I wonder
if the boys are facing a future goodness

that I cannot yet imagine
or the catastrophes that I can.

*

Philosophers say that when we feel awe,
the self becomes small. We realize

the world will go on with or without us,
and this knowledge is a kind of solace.

Once, I jogged past the Hajjar School
and the old tracks that connect Lowell

to Boston. The blast of the Concord River
roared past the mill that had once clothed a nation

and the remains of the old canal
that hovered like a spirit in the woods.

Thoreau was unimpressed by that once-great
miracle of innovation, how it created

a want of harmony in its scenery, but he
also observed that *in the lapse of ages,*

Nature will recover and indemnify herself.
Indemnify: to free from, or clear of, loss

or hurt. Thoreau was right: that morning,
I saw how the leaves, abundant and voluptuous,

bent toward and concealed everything
they touched—aqueduct, lock, bank, branch—

until I saw a world, not without us, exactly,
but certainly without us at the center.

*

Here on Nickerson Beach, hundreds
of oystercatchers crowd the bluffs.

Their orange bills and red eyes flare in the haze
as they mate and thus insist on their own existence.

It wasn't always so: in the Gilded Age,
they nearly vanished because of human folly

and desire—those black and white plumes,
those speckled eggs—but now they are so populous,

and so confident, that they swoop
and graze my head when I walk back

to the rows of pink and turquoise cabanas,
vestiges of an aluminum past.

*

Long before humans irretrievably altered air
and earth and sea, back when the eye of god

saw all things and humans dreaded that gazing,
during the history of our fear and the language

with which we tried to assemble and capture it,
the word *awe* was aligned with *eye*, god

watching us, marking all human choice
and movement with his terror. No need

for that god, now that every room of the mind
fills with terrors of our own making.

*

Tonight, as we eat from a plate filled with mussels,
George asks: *What will we say when our kids are grown*

and they wonder whether to have children on an earth
that is dying? At the end of the table, the kids

take photos of each other with our cellphones,
then walk among the restaurant's picnic benches

and faux palm trees. At first, the question seems funny—
Margaret jokes, *Why would they ever ask us*

about anything?—but the longer we spin
on the question, the harder it is to respond.

*

Between 1606 and 1610, Shakespeare wrote
his greatest plays, but the theaters of London

were open for a total of just nine months.
During that time, he wrote about lovesickness,

political turmoil, the curative power of music,
and the trials of old age, but almost nothing

about the quiet that shrouded the empty theaters,
the bubonic plague erupting and then receding

into a kind of understory, on and off, sometimes
for years during his own life, and for centuries

before and after. We say *renaissance* now,
but how could they have seen it as a time

of anything but demise and ruin? How could I
have read and not understood the crushing blows

of lost hours, the desperation of a word
like *pestilence*, the simple desire to be close

to others and live long enough to write
about that closeness? During the plague years,

people would walk the streets holding oranges
to their noses. They knew it wasn't a cure,

but the warmth of that smell in a cold, rainy place
and the flash of color amidst all of that darkness

must have been a kind of beauty. Of course,
the world we love will end, and this is only one

of many extinctions, but maybe we can remind
the children about those walks with oranges,

these rows of cabanas, these busy oystercatchers,
these ocean waves that persist in their unfolding,

the sheer momentum of all things, and my desire
to replicate that momentum, here, for you.

Ixion at the Museo del Prado

—after Jusepe de Ribera

Unknown source, endless suffering:
there is no light like this
anywhere on earth. Still, Ribera

approximates what is possible
in his painting of Ixion, the proud giant
who, after trying to seduce

Hera, was condemned to turn
upon a wheel of fire for all of eternity.
To notice requires some discomfort—

there's the stiffness in my neck
as I look up, and then
the claustrophobic closeness

of Ixion to the satyr who tortures him,
and the strangeness of the painting's
orientation. My eyes expect

the golden ratio, with the largest parts
of Ixion's body—the sinewed shoulders,
the powerful fist, the back tensed

with exertion—arriving at the bottom
of the painting. But no, Ribera's
signature indicates that he wants

a horizontal orientation, so that
Ixion's body can curve across the top
of the canvas, and beneath him,

the torturer can brace for whatever
    comes next. This way, too,
the light can play upon each rib

    in Ixion's back, on every furrow
in his brow, and while only part
    of his face is illuminated, one

can see he is not young—
    mottled skin, receding hairline,
crow's feet around the eyes.

    To read the art historians,
you might think Ribera was a hack—
    one critic described a disorderly life;

another dismissed the stock figures
    in his paintings—the instruments,
the punishers, the largeness of the bodies

    in pain, and his ceaseless repetition
of these tropes—as a way
    to make money and thus satisfy

his creditors. But what if Ribera
    was trying to understand pain
and its space, its time, its demands?

    Perhaps, with the sprawl
of his arms and legs pulled
    through eternity, even Ixion

might acknowledge that the pain
    has some value. He might
envision himself as the container

for all disasters of desire
with a suffering so large
that just by example, all torture

could come to an end. Or—
and this is more likely—what if
the enormity of the canvas

suggests that only the wealthiest
of Spaniards could have commissioned it,
that the painting is a reminder

of what befalls those who dare
to transgress that boundary
between gods and men,

the punishment a source
of pleasure for the tyrants who relied
on the permanence of that line.

The Birth of Venus

When I look at Botticelli's painting,
I see the arrival of all pleasure
and the desire for more of it.

I am arrested by the benevolence
of Zephyr and Aura, how they
anticipate Venus's need

for warm breezes and fallen blossoms,
and Hora, who nearly floats
with the lightness of the blanket

that she offers for modesty.
And then there is
Venus's hair—long,

lustrous copper shining
and then coiling down
and around her naked body—

a reminder of her souvenir
on Earth, that most ductile
and malleable of elements.

The word *copper* comes from *cuprum*,
for the frothy waters
off the coast of Cyprus

from which Venus emerged,
fully formed in all her radiance
and for the copper

that banked every shore.
In ancient times, it was said
that copper flowed from the veins

of her hot planet and all through
the universe, then down
into this world governed

by our hunger for the elemental.
When Alexander Graham Bell,
second only to Thomas Edison

in his appetites, first saw
what copper could do,
he scoured the world

for its quicksilver properties.
For Bell's deaf mother,
piano keys sounded

like a dull rumble,
and every voice
was an underwater pulse

that he sought to exhume.
He could almost imagine,
as if in a fever dream,

the sound of so many voices
reaching across great networks
of copper wire,

the Mediterranean warmth
of Cyprus in every private home,
the connections between

and among us like a filigree
canvassing the world.
Yes to connection, yes

to the human voice,
but the networks
are so fragile, so easy to destroy.

Today, on Amtrak,
I watch the rusted blur
of foreclosed houses

rise like tombs
throughout the prairie,
dead shells stripped

of the very connective tissue
that wed their inhabitants
to the world. Copper,

the thread connecting phone
to body, circuit board to body,
house to body, this godless need.

Bell Work

—after Atsuko Tanaka's *Work (Bell)* (1955)

What is the matter?
What is sound but matter,
not abstraction but wave
over or through
a solid thing,
pressure that ripples
from bell to ear,
as when the diaphragm
on the first phonograph
fluttered with movement,
then settled into grooves
on wax. As when,
a century later,
protesters were stunned
by peals that chirped
from sound cannons
beyond the range
of human cognition:
alien birds,
warbles of madness.

In an art gallery
on a sunny day,
years after
the war,
Tanaka strung a row
of bells around
the room, then left
an innocuous message
by the entrance—
Please push the button—
and the result,

not an angelic ring
but serious matter,
an emergency of sound,
mushroom clouds,
bull's eyes,
concentric radioactivity
shaped, occasionally,
like hearts
drawn to scale
after an implosion,
a sequence that frayed
the nerves of everyone
in the gallery,
especially the one
who pushed
the button first.

Excalibur

In the office of the genetics specialist,
        I climb on to the table and recite
the wish from the Metta Bhavana:
        May I be well; may I be happy; may I be free

from suffering. May you be well; may you
        be happy; may you be free from suffering.
When the doctor enters the tiny room,
        we offer greetings and compliment

his shiny shoes. He looks and says,
        Yes. They're called Excaliburs, then dims
the lights for the examination. Hard
        to imagine why a shoe company

would choose such a name for a product
        when there are so many other
magical swords in the world, like this:
        the Phillips Vaginal Transducer,

a marvel of technology, now even more marvelous
        in the hands of the doctor, especially
when he offers it to Jay and says,
        Would you like to help with the exam?

His offer politely declined, the doctor
        inserts the wand. We watch the monitor
for a jerk or bounce of a fetus,
        and there it is, glowing and throbbing,

a dream of cells assembling into organ systems.
        The doctor searches for what technology
knows to find: the too-small knob
        at the neck, the irregularities in the spine.

Later, he will send the blood sample
        to the lab workers who will search
for chromosomes that look
        like faraway islands surrounded

by dragons on a medieval map.
        The etymon is *chromos*, which sounds
like a god but comes from the Greek
        for *two colors*—the brilliant flare in every one

of its metallic compounds—and *soma,*
        body, the metals, colors, coiling,
spindling. Minutes of silence,
        and then the doctor says, *Everything is fine.*

II.

Septimania

—Barcelona

When I check to see which exit I should use
when emerging from the Lesseps Metro stop,
the map says *Septimania*, and instead of thinking
of that ancient borderland that once existed
between France and Spain, I remember
the septic tank at the center of my childhood
backyard, the contents of which were so full
of our excrement that our grass glowed
emerald green for decades until the town managers
decided to create whole rivers of putrefaction
streaming underneath the road into sewage systems
that would have made the ancient Romans proud.
I take Septimania, emerge from the bowels
of the earth, walk 290 meters, and arrive
at the door of my son's preschool
where he has been baking bread for the past hour.
There's something so precious about the lightness
of that activity, all that leavening and rising,
that I laugh when the headmaster tells me
about three-year-olds baking bread every day.
He looks at me and says, *Why are you laughing?*
The bread is delicious! Yes, headmaster,
yes to lightness and rising, even if
I needed to wade through putrefaction
to get to it. Excrement has become all the rage—
one day of news from America is enough
to convince anyone of that. It seems, though,
that war has always been a magnet for fundament.
Just today, I was rereading George Orwell's
Homage to Catalonia and I marveled
at his attention to diarrhea, decaying food,
and the horse dung of the Spanish Civil War.

Later, I learned from Adam Hochschild
that the women who belonged to unions and yearned
for a classless society were objects of such enmity
that everything needed to be taken from them.
Sometimes the soldiers took their newborns;
sometimes Franco's soldiers tattooed
the women's flesh with the yoke and arrows
of the Falangists; sometimes the soldiers
gang-raped the women and then bragged
to anyone who would listen; sometimes,
if the women still resisted, they
were forced to drink castor oil, a powerful
laxative, and then parade through the streets,
being jeered as they soiled themselves. Today
is another beautiful day, radiant with Mediterranean
sun, even in January. My son and I walk
to Plaça del Diamant, the site of the old
air-raid shelter, and a bronze statue of a woman
whose naked body seems to rise and break
through the earth. At first, her pose suggests
that she is an emblem of freedom, but no.
Her stance is one of both terror and amazement.
The bronze eviscerates her body, breaking it
in two. In the plaza, we do what all
the other families do: play "crazy car"
with his balance bike, buy candy at the supermercat,
then descend again into the underworld
of the Metro, as if everyone knows
what happened here, and who belonged to whom.

The Purity Instinct

Near the end, Ceausescu would only drink juice
through a straw. Twice, he was convinced
that his hearing had improved: once when he heard
the sound of a distant train from his youth;
and again when his long-dead mother sang
a little-known song in his ear. Other times—
orange was especially good for this—he felt
his bones straighten, and once, after a tall glass
of grapefruit, his arms acquired the strong sinews
of his time as the village shepherd and shoemaker.
With prunes, his skin became impervious to cold.
At a banquet held in his honor, he walked
to the balcony, stood in the rain, and did not shiver once.
On the road, his assistant kept all the straws
in a satchel; at home, every drawer was full of them.
On the first of each month, a crate went directly
to the kitchen built with the blood of traitors
and the money of the West. After a childhood
of pig fat and sheep's milk and filth all around,
the purity instinct was strong for Ceausescu.
In those final moments, as he sang
The Internationale, his hands cuffed to his wife's,
he must have admired how clean the bullet was
in its chamber, the singular force of its straight line.

Shotgun, Rabies

Better to die than disobey:
    that's the lesson
my father-in-law conveyed
    when he told the story
of his brother's miserable end.
    I imagine that brother
from the last century,
    and the moment
at which his ordinary life
    was made extraordinary
by the dog's spittle
    and sway, the lolling head,
the slow approach,
    the pain of the bite,
the terror in the dog's
    frantic eyes; then the boy's
fear of water on an island
    comprised of more water
than air; then the sternness
    of a father who didn't want
to know the truth
    if it meant that his son
had trespassed
    and disobeyed.
For me, that brother's death
    was a lesson in chaos,
how it whips children
    into the air until
they are hot, distant stars,
    so far beyond our control,
almost unrecognizable
    when their disasters occur,

and that the disasters
    are so frequent,
and so proximate, even here,
    in a town best known
for its salted peanuts
    and insurance policies.
Yesterday, a couple
    brought their pet capuchin
to play at Franklin Park,
    just a block away.
Locals watched
    as the small monkey swung
from one swing to another,
    groveled in the sand,
then hurled his own feces
    as he inched down the slide.
Today, as I walked
    past the park, I saw
a grandmother pushing
    her grandchild
on one of the swings,
    the baby's hands
squeezing the links.
    What use in telling
what had happened?
    Across the park, one can see
the famous Stevenson home
    where Adlai was raised
until, at twelve,
    he pointed a rifle
at his neighbor
    and, without knowing

it was loaded, pulled
    the trigger and killed her
instantly. Further down Route 66,
    past the empty sausage tins
and crushed straws and food banks,
    past the storage facilities and a freight train
so long and slow
    that it nearly drags
the town with it
    is Adlai Stevenson's gravesite.
The tombs of his nearest relatives
    encircle a cool white stone,
bare except for their last name,
    dates of birth and death,
and a plaque that summarizes
    his public accomplishments:
governor of Illinois,
    presidential hopeful, ambassador
to the United Nations.
    No mention of the violence
that undid his youth,
    the ripples that tore
through that young girl's family,
    the one he never meant
to destroy. This week,
    his story thrummed
with an electric charge
    when a nine-year-old girl
accidentally shot and killed
    her firearms instructor
at a shooting range in Nevada.
    What will she feel some day—
perhaps when studying
    for an exam, or preparing
for travel, or watching

a monkey on a swing
at a local park, when she learns
that *rabies* comes from the Sanskrit
for *to do violence,*
and that an animal
will thrive inside her
for the rest of her days.

The Ghost Workers

The fountain on Bonifacio High Street
    begins as a bubble and ends as a perfect arch.
The children feel just a sprinkle

    then run, all appetite and thirst,
into each of the small spigots
    while passersby marvel at the colors

and shadows, long and sensuous,
    that relax each person's face
until all sorrow vanishes

    in the rhythms of the automation.
At this time of day, one might imagine
    that Bonifacio High Street is any place

in the secular West: Seurat's *Le Grande Jatte,*
    a postcard of the Bethesda Fountain
at the turn of the last century,

    Childe Hassam's *Boston Common at Twilight,*
but everything here is bright and new.
    If you were to search for this part of Manila

in a guidebook published before 2013,
    you would not find it. My mother-in-law
remembers it as Fort McKinley;

    younger locals remember it as a barangay
of Taguig; and now, it is Bonifacio Global City.
    The developers of the new Manila

would have expats believe
    that BGC rose from nothing, free
of history, an erasure of the political prison

    and the barracks abandoned by the Americans
after World War II. Most days, Jay leaves early
    to photograph the families

left behind by the mothers and fathers
    who migrate to Hong Kong, Dubai,
and Singapore, sometimes for years,

    working in the shadows so their children
can thrive. My son's balloon wobbles
    as we race across the intersections

that connect us to a fantasy world
    of fountains and malls and condos. At first,
we were surprised by the cranes that never stop,

    the rebar and wet cement, the men
from the provinces who ride buses for hours
    in order to toil, men wearing long sleeves

and towels on their heads to protect them
    from the midday heat, these Tondo men,
Quiapo men, thin as the wires they install

    all over the city, men whose accidental deaths
never seem to count. My dad calls them
    the ghost workers. For days during his visit,

he watched them from the window
    of our apartment on the seventeenth floor,
all of them swinging from scaffolding

    without as much as a helmet to protect them
when they fell. *They're like the coal miners*
    in Lewis Hine's photo, he says, *the ones who have death*

in their eyes. Every day, curtains of sheer netting
    drift above our heads to protect us
from the small bits of sub-par concrete

    and wires that will fry every electrical device.
Cement mixers and pickup trucks full of men
    enter and exit through corrugated metal walls,

and if you peek through the cracks, you can see
    the actors—of industry, of dust. Every day
ends with the crepuscular radiance

    that makes all mistakes seem smaller,
and the knowledge that the rebar will vanish
    beneath a patina of glossy stone. Anyone looking

    for an emblem of globalization, that grandchild
of empire, should look to those who fall
    to their deaths to strengthen its foundation.

Equator Sky, Manila Bay

Here, the brightest constellation
  is Hydra, the Water Snake, named
for the half-woman, half-reptile

  whom Hercules slew with the help
of Iolaus, his charioteer. Imagine
  the sound of so many heads screaming—

the long, shrill bays of an angry woman
  times twenty—and the smell of birth,
of all origins, that followed Hydra

  as she rose from her fetid swamp. Iolaus
was strategic, went straight for the bowels
  instead of the mouth, burned her center

before the head. When her fundament
  was reduced to ash, only then could
Hydra be silenced. Hera, enraged

  that Hercules was able to slay the creature
she had raised in order to destroy him,
  flung the corpse of the decapitated,

maimed Hydra into the sky, lest she be
  forgotten. Hydra's blood, unstoppable,
became hot gas; her screams rose

  and fell until they were radio waves;
and her wild flailing was fixed
  into points of light. Hera was right

to hurl those stars here, above this bay,
   so close to where the earth bisects,
a place where Hydra's mirror image

   glosses the water, where dense blooms
of algae flourish on the nitrogen surface,
   thousands of wild heads and arms

devouring ammonia, cyanide, and sewage
   as fast as we can produce them,
this hydra, emblem of insatiable desire.

Crossing Tsing Ma Bridge

—Hong Kong

I'm wed to the pain, the ugly, the monstrous,
the criminal, and I am the enemy of beauty,
except in rare cases, like tonight, when I cross
the Tsing Ma Bridge for the first time.
Maybe this can be the one exception in which grace
shimmers in the tiny red lights that dot the tops
of high-rise monoliths and constellate
the broad expanse of the Ma Wan Channel.
The other riders on the coach bus, silhouettes
still as stones, are silent for the entire ride,
suspended by an engineering marvel and a feeling
of awe for a city, so new and yet so old, built
upon a foundation of movable goods,
movable people, everything in a state
of constant migration. This doubleness
of pain and beauty, and the feeling of suspension
from both, is as rare as the pink dolphins
of the Pearl River, as difficult to navigate
as the dark water beneath us. For just a few minutes
as we cross the bridge, we have no bodies but eyes,
no brains but stems, breathing and pulsing in the dark.

Psychomachia

—Manila

At the Mind Museum, you can walk to the back,
step on several large buttons on the ground,

and watch parts of the brain light up: the frontal cortex
for decision and memory, the temporal lobe

for smell and sound, the occipital for sight. I try
to make my toddler son laugh by hopping

from one button to the next, watching each lobe
light up along the way, but he will not leave the prison

of his melancholy. My son: how he loves to revisit
the most difficult point of conflict in a picture book,

or the moment at which his favorite car heaves
a sigh at the pinnacle of a movie's emotional

arc, or the promise of injury if I take a fall. My son,
so distant from other children in his sadness.

Just the other day, at the pool, he gazed
at the boys and girls splashing and shrieking

and said, *Look. The children are having fun,*
as if he were an anthropologist in a foreign land.

If these are his musings at age two, one can only
imagine the life that must follow. Through a dark channel

he was born; to darkness he is most drawn. My son, always
in the world without husk or shell, it is as if his heart

throbs on the outside of his body, as if his brain
has no skull to absorb the assaults that strike it.

Today, I watch him writhe in the pain of a tantrum—
a typical kid, this is what they do, everyone assures

me—and usually I rush in, unwittingly increasing
his sense of emergency. Instead, today, I stand back,

relinquish the role of skull and skin, watch his mind
unfurl like a medieval tapestry. In that moment

of my feigned disinterest, his head is no longer head
but battlefield where Wrath wages a fierce war

against Patience. He is no longer a little boy
screaming on the ground and throwing plastic trucks;

instead he is a creature engaged in a struggle
to free his *enslaved heart* from the monsters

whose foaming mouths and *hot fumes*
and *clots of foul blood* have besieged him

as he gathers his thoughts from the unraveling
of his universe. Prudentius says that *fiery Wrath*

in her frenzy slays herself and dies
by her own weapons. I will watch and wait

for my son to close his mind from the anger
and sorrow that fester in him, but if the mind

does not close, I hope I can hide the weapons
before, one day, it is too late.

The Ovid Room

When my four-year-old son lists a few
of the sixty-seven moons of Jupiter—
Io, Europa, Ganymede, Leda—
and the space probe *Juno* that surveils

them at all times, I remember
Federico Gonzaga, the Mantuan duke
who, in the 1530s, created an Ovid Room
in his Palazzo de Te. He was like

that one suburban neighbor who's always
the first to get a giant 4K television,
the one who scores the in-ground pool
with the margarita bar in the middle,

but in a world without TVs
or margaritas, Federico chose
to create a *Sala di Ovidio* in which all
four walls and the ceiling would be covered

with friezes and paintings depicting
the most famous "scenes of love"
from Ovid's *Metamorphoses*. And I'm thinking
what you're thinking: Love? When

did Ovid ever say anything about that?
Abduction, rape, murder: those
are the subjects of nearly every poem
that Ovid wrote. Federico's got his own

angle on things, as does Antonio da Correggio,
the painter whom he has commissioned
to make the work. Jove's rape of Io, daughter
of Inachus, is a case in point. We know

that after Jove assaulted the young girl,
he turned her into a cow so that jealous Juno
would never find her. In Ovid's text,
"he took her," as if she were an item

in the lost and found bin; and in the painting,
Io's long, naked back is illuminated
by a strange light, perhaps a sun obscured
by a cloud or fog, and she sits on a draped piece

of white cloth, and the toes on her left foot
are curled as if to suggest that the feeling
is mutual, which of course it isn't
and could never be. Italo Calvino

casually remarked that Ovid
revealed the *interpenetration of gods, men,*
and nature, as if that were a productive thing,
all that chasing and transgressing, exile

and oblivion. Federico asked for a whole room
of such paintings—not of Io hobbled
and haltered, Ganymede in servitude,
Danae's panic in a locked cabinet

tossing on the seas; but Jove
as both god and swan, leading the girls
aside and away. When my son asks
for the stories behind the many moons,

the lonely satellite, I read
from my favorite English translation,
and when *rape* metamorphoses into *taken,*
I repeat the beautiful, ravishing lie.

Poolside

I would never hit a woman. Funny
what people will tell you while waiting
for a thundershower to end. The rain
falls hard on the water, leaping back up
in daggers while my son and I stand
in the vestibule between the pool
and parking lot, my son who would still
rather hang onto my back than blow bubbles,
who would rather grab me from behind
and drive me like a car through the water,
who still doesn't quite know where his own body ends
and mine begins. A man waits with us
in this vestibule, pool water still dripping down
his legs, scars from a recent surgery still dotting
his shoulder as he casually feeds potato chips
to the children who stand with him. They take
the bag of chips and offer it to my son.
He takes one and looks out the window
to watch the heavy clouds roll across the sky.
Out of nowhere, I learn that these children
are not the man's—he eagerly tells me that—
they are his son's kids, and now he
takes care of them, and yes, there was
a time when he and his wife were together,
and a time when she cheated on him,
and a time when he confronted her
in front of his then-young sons, and I feel myself
doing now what I always do, what we
are trained to do from the earliest age,
I'm leaning in, I'm showing care in my eyes,
I've been convinced when I've seen this look
on my face in old photos so I know it's working

and it works when other women do it, too,
and after all, the lifeguard just said
that it will be at least another fifteen minutes
before we can go back to the pool,
and this man loves his sons, there's no doubt
of that, he's got that attempted tattoo
on his arm, which was apparently so painful
that the tattoo artist had to stop
after the first three letters of one son's name.
I would never hit a woman, he says. *It's cowardly.*
If you want to do that, go out and find a man
to hit. At least that's a fair fight, and yes, of course
I follow the logic, I know the work of empathy.
But when she slapped me, I hit her hard,
and to demonstrate the effect, he hits me
on the arm, there in the waiting area, and yes,
a demonstration is helpful, I can imagine
the scenario, and I want to follow the story
to its logical end, but when my son says
I have to go potty of course I must attend
to this biological need. Later, once
we've driven away, I assume that my son
has been untouched by anything the man
has said, busy as he was staring at the rain,
at the children playing. That night,
I recalled the encounter at the dinner table,
and when I asked my son if he remembered
the man, he said, *You mean the one who punched you?*

Electrolux

I turn the earth
more clay than soil
and exhume an Alton brick,
a heavy reminder
that only a few miles
south of here
one finds magnolia trees,
a humid climate,

and the subtropical confluence
of the Illinois
and Mississippi Rivers,
that gateway
to both escape and riot.
Here, though,
the earth dries in black cracks.
Coneflower,
sedum,
bee balm,
salvia:
all attempts
to bring monarchs,
bees,
hummingbirds,
migrants bulking up
on nectar
before their primordial flight
to Central America
and beyond.

For hours I pull
hair-like roots,
networks of crab grass,
white, prehistoric grubs,
rusty nails,
and then I wash
all of my clothes
in our Electrolux
washing machine.
Lux for light, white,
bright…
spin cycle.
For decades,
the Electrolux headquarters
stood on the corner
where Main meets Walnut.
Before that, the site
was home
to the Mennonite Sanitarium
which included
a surgical suite,
the autoclave room,
an eye bank,
a child care center,
and a birthing room
which, in 1918,
welcomed George Lincoln Rockwell,
founder
of the American Nazi Party.

Now
it is an empty lot
that faces
an out-of-business gas station
that fueled
the dream
of Route 66,
which today is just a distant fume.
Our new garden
is kidney-shaped,
a figure eight.
The sprinkler ticks away
the hours
during which
the black cracks
will join with peat
to create earth
that is habitable.
Later, I stare
at the water
in my frontloading washer
as it rises
to submerge
the soiled clothes
and I remember
my days in laundromats
before buying this machine,
the perfume of fabric softener
strong as sweat.
As the earth
gets hotter,
we go to public pools,
cold ripples of chlorine
killing every germ
in the kiddie splash pool.

Just a few inches
of water is enough
to sit down
or crawl on all fours
and race like a crab
to catch my son.
As we approach
the tiny water slide,
we arrive at a man
sitting by the pool's edge
with a baby.
He sports a sleeve
of tattoos on each arm:
a German flag,
an Iron Cross,
SS bolts of lightning,
the hand gesture
that once meant *ok*
but now
also means *white power,*
and the Wolfsangel,
ancient runic symbol
meant to protect
the wearer from wolves.
I crawled
toward his body
which registered first
as father
then as Nazi
and saw that he
was not alone,
that other fathers
were with him,
covered
with ancient appropriations,

and I wondered
which algorithm
they might be using
to rank my son's skin.
Later, when
I told a friend,
she wasn't surprised.
In 1974,
George Lincoln Rockwell
was murdered
by one of his own
outside of a laundromat,
and after his death,
American Nazis
came to town
to lay a wreath
by his birthplace
and march in the street.
The marches fizzled
once Electrolux
bought the land.
My Electrolux, though,
is a marvel.
The whites are whiter
than I've ever seen,
but there is no joy here,
no way to talk happily
of washing and whiteness.

Electrocuting an Elephant

—after Raúl Martínez Beteta

At the Museu Marítim Barcelona, I stood
    in the entryway and watched the automaton:
a dull metal fish that swung and rotated
    without any apparent assistance

save for the push of air that my presence
    brought to it. The steel was an orange shimmer
of underwater motion; the sky above glowed
    topaz like the Mediterranean; and the fish,

larger than life, swung its creaky tail
    from one side to another with a sound
of recycled metals and nails and nets,
    junk from the sea that would and does kill

any real ocean life, now repurposed
    and born again. The fish hearkened back
to a Renaissance desire for things
    that move as if on their own, so lively,

so animated with a kind of spirit,
    that they might even be capable of emotion.
When the spring is pushed, the machine stirs,
    just like the human body with its various clocks

that chime throughout the day.
    Who knows how much of any being
is sheer will, and how much pure inertia.
    Take Topsy, for example. When I first read

about this spectacularly troubled elephant,
    it was in the context of Edison's great
experiment: his way of assuring the world
    that direct current was superior to alternate,

that its shock would be swift, clean, and painless.
    Topsy's rage was her primary emotion.
By the time she was electrocuted, she had already killed
    a man, attacked several others, and her death

was, in the view of her owners, inevitable,
    no matter that the man she killed had goaded her
with lit cigarettes and booze and heckling.
    When you've got a bad elephant

on your hands, the thinking went,
    there was nothing to do but send a charge
through its body, and if the death
    were in service to modern electricity,

progress, and change, then all the better.
    In the moments before Topsy died,
it almost seemed like the cyanide-laced carrots
    and her slow walk in copper slippers

were a part of the elephant's wish, a last great bow
    that only she could initiate. I look again at the fan
of the fish's tail, its creak and glide, how it opens
    to all possibility, which is a machine of its very own.

Why I Haven't Written

—after Marcel Bénabou

1.

Because it's 5 a.m. and I would rather watch
the ashy tip of Jean-Luc Godard's clove cigarette

nearly fall onto the beige carpet of Dick Cavett's
TV studio, just as he introduces the clip

from his newest film *Every Man for Himself,*
and then the clip itself: A cluttered, too-close

kitchen scene where the young man quietly reads
a thin magazine then says aloud, *"100 Do-It-Yourself*

Ideas," my God! and then he puts down the paper,
his fork quietly touches the plate, and he stares

at his girlfriend, who's staring at her fingers, then
at him with a look that suggests pure contempt,

or boredom, or both, and when he says *I've got*
an idea, she says, *You?* as if she has only known him

to be an idiot, a caveman, and then he becomes
that caveman, leaping across the kitchen table,

spilling the dishes as he pounces on her,
and then the film slows as they both careen

toward the floor, as their heads just miss
the broom in the dusty corner, as they wrap

their arms around each other's necks,
as they land on the tiles. Her face betrays

what seems to be a smile, but it's a wince,
too, a preparation for the fall that will inevitably injure

the actress, even if the camera keeps rolling,
and then, after a full minute of the clenching

and grasping in the slowest motion possible,
he gets up and leaves her on the floor.

When he says *We can't seem to touch without bruising,*
he's looking at her as he walks away, there

in the doorway, just before he goes outside
to take a walk, with a look full of both longing

and hatred, the two feelings utterly inseparable,
a look that is remarkable for how familiar it is.

2.

Because I would rather contemplate
Mary Shelley during the poverty year.
The summer that never was. The dry fog.
The weather backward, barren like winter.
The Frankenstein summer when her half-sister
died by suicide. The last season of her son's
short life. The summer of no food, of ice
in every tree, of no sun. Now, we know:
it was volcanic ash. But then, she thought
Little Ice Age, England's Dark Day,
miscarriage, mother dying in childbirth, a year
when the earth stood still in its own rupture.

3.

—after Auguste Clésinger's *Woman Bitten by a Snake*

Because the openness of it scandalized viewers
at the 1847 Salon of Paris; because Clésinger chose

to mold the plaster from a cast placed all around
the woman's body; because her backside revealed

the dimples of Venus, and her thighs the light brush
of cellulite; because she wore the snake around her arm

like a bracelet, a kind of reward; because she was so
available to anyone's view, so promiscuous, so…*free*;

because for Clésinger her creation wasn't painful;
the cast was a cheat, required no patience,

no suffering; because despite all of this talk
of counterfeit ease and excess luxury, the electricity

that rose from within seemed enough
to light a bulb, though dimly, and with a flicker.

4.

—after *AAA-AAA* (1978)

Because I would rather watch Marina Abramovic
shouting at Ulay, both of them young and wild,

the monotone brays of animals hurled
into the channel between their bodies, no words,

no change in facial expression, just volume and pitch
escalating with each new breath in the low-fi

analog of black-and-white film; because
when they start, I think performance artists,

acting, ornament, superficial, shallow, thin,
and then, by the time they arrive at the fourth minute,

I think why did he sleep with his translator,
why did she get pregnant, when

did Abramovic find out, does she know
as she wails with her mouth an inch away from his

that he will be the source of her central pain,
that she will be ruined by him for decades,

long after they say goodbye at the Great Wall
of China, the goodbye that in and of itself

is a performance, a thorough completion,
until, of course, many years later, when she

is utterly alone in a room with dozens
of museumgoers who watch as she sits

in a bright red dress to gaze at anyone
who will face her at the table. Some cry; some

look away; one touches his hand to his heart,
disarmed by the complete attention Abramovic offers

to every single person, by the idea that she could do it,
not for days or hours but months, her face a mask,

waxlike, of pure presence, almost a mirror, until,
of course, Ulay walks to the chair opposite hers.

While her eyes are closed, he adjusts his long legs
under the table, lowers his shoulders, and stares

so that when she opens her level eyes, her mouth
widens and her skin emanates a light that has nothing

to do with the electric gels above their heads.
She smiles, then weeps. Only silence now

as she reaches for his hands, and then, after
a single touch, he leaves as easily as he arrived.

A Thousand Flowers

Arthur Rubloff Collection of Paperweights,
Art Institute of Chicago

The history of America
  is the history of the blowtorch

and the propane gas
  that molds the skyscrapers

that rise on the hottest days
  of summer. It is the hubris

that coats the plain façade
  of the Page Brothers Building,

built just one year
  after the great fire that melted

cast iron buildings
  into mountains of lava

so hot and fast
  that the people's only refuge

was to run to the lake
  and stand in its waters

until the land had cooled.
  It is the stubbornness

that it takes to forge
  from that same material

even when you know
  its brittleness, even when

the city is a testament
  to ruin. It is the need

for open windows
  on those insufferable top floors,

and then another need
  for glass paperweights

on every desk covered
  with piles of papers—

for pigs, for cows, for dairy,
  for trains, for more

skyscrapers—about to be
  blown and scattered

across the desolation
  of the prairie. It is

the thousand glass flowers
  that fix all of those papers

in place: cross-sections
  of bundled roses, fruits,

and snakes, bullets
  of color, the heft

of lead glass, the illusion
  of depth; and sometimes,

it is a glass salamander
    luxuriating on the top

of the paperweight
    like a rotten weed

born of fire, a black slick
    glistening,

waiting for its prey;
    a messenger

carrying the ash
    of the spent world.

The Face

With a small knife, Catherine scrapes
the last daubs of paint from her palette:
not color so much as confusion, from *confound,*
from the Latin *confundere,* to mingle, mix up,
pour. Earlier today, she painted a study of me
reading on the patio, my back to her, one side
of my face partly visible, my left hand hovering
above my hair, two fingers up, two fingers scratching
as I grapple with the most painful lines
of *King Lear,* when Gloucester, eyes gouged out,
walks to the precipice, certain of death
with each step. *I have no way, and therefore want*
no eyes. Catherine keeps scraping as we talk,
her grip surgical, forensic. When done,
she covers each mingled color with plastic wrap.
I marvel at her desire to salvage what's left,
and she says *Well, that's the fun, isn't it?*
Finding out which colors will be there
for tomorrow. And it's true: her palette
is the trace of her imagination
from one day to the next. The mind,
even when at its best, is more residue
than substance, more shadow than fact.

Her palette reminds me of the self-portraits
of William Utermohlen, all from the time
when his mind was in the midst of its own removal.
In one painting, right after the diagnosis,
the vanishing begins as a look of recalcitrance,
but as the plaque continues its clot
and tangle through every cell, his face
becomes a sooty smear, eyes gouged

like Gloucester's, body surrounded
by a tempest full of grit and sand and ash
as he faces the cliff's wild edge. He painted
with perfect vision but could not remember
his own eyes. Only sockets now,
front lobe, sparse hair, line for a mouth,
cylinder for a neck, and yet, there they are:
the grooves of grief, the anguish of evasion.

III.

Electric Dress

—after Atsuko Tanaka's *Electric Dress* (1956)

When she wears the dress, she becomes
  the most ductile, malleable, circuited,
and encircled of all women. She doesn't know

  what 4,000 watts will do when she inserts
the cord into the socket, and in truth
  she'd rather be electrocuted

than merely vanish like the man
  caught on the bank's front steps
on the day of the attack, his radioactive shadow

  hovering for years after the end of the war.
In this dress, she is more intricate
  than the crisscross pattern

that seared the back of one small girl,
  more powerful than the aftereffects
of vomit, hair loss, skin burns,

  and radiation clinging to the soil.
Tonight, she is her own power source,
  her own attempted suicide, her own

emergency response. She is all progress,
  all future, all technology, no past,
the brightest living object in the room.

Cassini

Yesterday, I watched a Florentine
    create paper with the mineral spirits
        of acrylic paint, water, and glue.

He opened a shallow tank
    for liquids to congeal,
        gently tapped each paint

into the gel, swirled the end
    of a thin paintbrush up and down
        and across the tank, then lowered

a plain piece of paper
    into the bath. What rose
        was a metamorphosis: dozens

of peacocks radiating up and down
    the page, so vibrant, so close,
        that in those plumes I thought I heard

the prehistoric brays of dinosaurs
    traveling through time. How magnificent
        to watch a technique we no longer need,

to have a foreknowledge of our paper lives.
    Photography can do this, too:
        this year, in its grand finale, Cassini,

the magnificent space probe
    that has dipped and danced
        around and through the rings

of Saturn for thirteen years
    will dive twenty-two times
        through gas and ice to reveal

a system that is not cold and dark
    but full of stunning energy:
        water spewing in plumes

from the edge of a perforated moon;
    endless, Sahara-like dunes
        that span what could be continents;

and channels of liquid methane sludge
    that feather in every direction.
        In one, a pin-prick of light

glows next to Saturn, a dot so small
    that one might mistake it
        for a speck of dust on an otherwise

perfect composite photograph:
    Earth, where all our woes and strife
        are contained, pure white,

blemish-free. The photo does not show
    the edges of our nation as it is eaten
        by the president like a giant,

well-done steak; or the police
    who have been exonerated
        for every crime against a brown body;

or the fish depleted from the hungry shores
of China and Africa; or the thousands
who have drowned, without papers,

in those fishless waters as they flee
from the tyrannies of home.
Cassini has no use for that. It only

follows what it loves—namely,
Enceladus, the brightest object
in the solar system. Beneath

its veneer of fresh ice, liquid methane
swells and stirs as water might have
on planet Earth, before time began,

before radiance, dynamism, smallness,
and catastrophe, with a vision of what
we might have been before there was a *we*.

Every Planet Is a Greeting

I am from a place so icy and vast, so dark
    and unknown, that it's easy to forget
the meaning of closeness. In winter, the stubble
    of corn and soy reveals an emptiness in the land,
and the void between each farmhouse
    ensures social distance, even without a pandemic.
I can jog for miles at dusk, my only company
    the sound of my breath in my mask.

Above me, the magical conjunction of Jupiter and Saturn
    shimmers in the sky, and their almost-touch
for the first time in 800 years
    is so affectionate that it is painful to watch.
But not all is seclusion and remoteness; not all
    is beyond my reach. Recently, I learned
that a local astronomer created a scale model
    of the solar system that spans 6,000 square miles

of prairie, here in Central Illinois. Who does that?
    Who would want to bring us what we cannot
fathom here on Earth, amid wind farms
    and country roads? When I stand on the sun—
42 feet in diameter, a yellow splash of paint
    on the patio of the Peoria Riverfront Museum—
I am, briefly, at the center of the universe.
    Just a short stroll along the Illinois River

brings me to Mercury, winged messenger,
    most erratic in its orbit, now small as a golf ball
and motionless beside a playground swing.
    I walk a little further on the Pimiteoui Trail
and see Venus, full-figured as always

and nestled among naked birches and sycamores.
At the fork where two paths meet, Earth
is softball-sized, with an ominous inscription

on its plaque: *The planet hasn't always been*
hospitable for humans, and isn't guaranteed
to remain so. Down by the marina, near a boat
called *Knot a Problem,* Mars stands vigilant
near a gaggle of ornery geese. Travel
to the gas giants requires some planning,
but it's still so easy: a ten-minute drive from here,
Jupiter hangs in the lobby of the Peoria Airport,

and I don't even have to enter the doors
to see its giant red spot swirling in the front window.
Saturn is less conspicuous, drifting as it does
from the low ceiling of the children's reading room
in the Pekin Public Library. Uranus,
that cold ammonia custodian of the skies,
hovers on its side by an empty football field
in Princeville; and Neptune is a watery sapphire

above the paved trail that now conceals
the legendary Rock Island Line. I could not
neglect Pluto, exiled as it is from the planets now;
after all, my 8-year-old son's favorite T-shirt
reads *Never Forget: Pluto 1930-2006,* and he insists
that we visit Good's Furniture Store
in Kewanee to see the demoted dwarf planet,
tiny as a raisin, glued to a plaque right above

a charming sectional sofa and coffee table.
Pluto, named after the surly underworld god,
banished because it *has not cleared its neighboring region*
of other objects. Pluto's only flaw? It was born into seclusion,

and as a result, it welcomes every object into its world
    without judgment. It is the very best neighbor, its orbit
always an open door. For three days, we shuttled
    past closed storefronts and empty main streets,

no one else in sight for hours. How many others
    have wandered from one planet to the next as we have?
We only made this pilgrimage because
    there was nowhere else to go, no family or friends,
no laughter or kisses, handshakes or song. Right now,
    all we have is this interstellar travel, this brush with Pluto
who dares to draw the most distant objects close,
    this reminder that we too will find closeness again.

Losing Blue

[B]lue, to the Greeks, was a species of darkness.
—Philip Ball

Looms of color and curve, each long panel of fabric
waving like a new sound in the dirge
of the Anthropocene. In one print, gray bands,

ominous and lethal, surround turquoise waves:
Lake Zigadenus, the gem of Banff National Park,
its spectacular opacity so bright that I doubt

what I am seeing, but it is true: until recently
the lake was turquoise, the result of a glacial silt
that floats and glints in the sun. The lake is losing its blue

because of turbidity, its muddy violence,
which leads me to think of blue's
troubled past, the fact that no word

for *blue* seemed to exist among the Ancients,
but it's there, always there: even among the blind,
blue rays are the ones that are visible, and yet

the earliest words for *blue* in English were *livid, pale,*
leaden, bruised. What is it about blue that is so hard
to find, and then, once found, so easy to disregard?

To the right, in this same print, the Zigadenus flower
thrives on the glacier that feeds it—linear leaves,
graceful panicles of white, easy spread of calyx—

but even that beauty is a mistake, as the other name
for Zigadenus is *death camas,* wildflower
whose alkaline blossoms dazzle, stun, and kill.

Lavender

The air is alive with our failure.
—Deborah Digges

At first they might feel like a mistake,
these tiny shrubs, these sisters to mint

and weed, these lanceolate leaves,
these etymons of the plant's name

buried in laundry and funerary rites,
but then, in a flash, the world is all

Cezanne, all barn in a purple field,
and you climb to the second floor

and stand with your toes on the edge
to behold it: miles of cornstalks

punctuated by this profundity
of lavender. Half of you might think

world's end, sixth extinction, near apocalypse,
but the other half will wonder,

Where does the hair that whips across the face
become prairie, what is an acre

of lavender, what is this ache? Forty
can feel like days on water, a season

of penitence, years of exile. It is
composite, and like all such numbers,

only semi-perfect, but no harm done.
Sometimes it takes years to know

tenderness, which, as the word implies,
is its own form of currency.

Today, let the mind wander and fan
and even surrender to the body,

then walk through a field of lavender
on this edge of before and after.

Therein lies—believe it—a kind
of contentment, with the body

not a map or a clock but a sprig,
tightly bound, and full of vibrant matter.

Notes

"Illuminated" is a modified erasure of "Edison's Electric Light: 'The Times' Building Illuminated by Electricity," *New York Times*, September 5, 1882.

"Nickerson Beach": The italicized quote comes from Thoreau's *A Week on the Concord and Merrimack Rivers* (1849). The anecdote about the oranges comes from Stephen Greenblatt's "What Shakespeare Actually Wrote about the Plague," *New Yorker*, March 20, 2020.

"Septimania": The italicized phrases in this poem come from Adam Hochschild's *Spain in Our Hearts: Americans in the Spanish Civil War, 1936-1939* (Mariner Books, 2017).

"The Purity Instinct" is inspired by this episode of the *Dinner Party* podcast from December 11, 2014: www.dinnerpartydownload.org/dictator-dinners/

"Psychomachia": The italicized quotes come from H.J. Thomson's translation of Prudentius's *Psychomachia* (Harvard University Press, 1949).

"The Ovid Room": the italicized quote comes from Italo Calvino's *The Uses of Literature* (Harcourt Brace Jovanovich, 1986), p. 150.

"Electrocuting an Elephant": the italicized quotes come from Joseph Roach's anecdotes about René Descartes in *The Player's Passion* (University of Michigan Press, 1993), p. 62.

"Why I Have Not Written" is inspired by Marcel Bénabou's *Why I Have Not Written Any of My Books* (Bison Books, 1998).

"The Face" features quotes from William Shakespeare's *King Lear* and painter Catherine Drabkin, whose work can be found at: catherinedrabkin.com/.

"Every Planet Is a Greeting": the first italicized phrase comes from the plaque attached to planet Earth in Peoria. The second italicized phrase comes from Library of Congress Everyday Mysteries page: www.loc.gov/everyday-mysteries/astronomy/item/why-is-pluto-no-longer-a-planet/#:~:text=Answer,neighboring%20region%20of%20other%20objects.%E2%80%9D.

"Losing Blue": This poem was inspired by Alice Hargrave's "Conference of the Lakes" series. The epigraph comes from *Bright Earth: Art and the Invention of Color* (University of Chicago Press, 2001), p. 233.

"Lavender": The phrase "vibrant matter" comes from Jane Bennett's book of the same title (Duke University Press, 2010).

Acknowledgments

Thank you to the editors of the publications in which some of these poems have appeared, sometimes in different form:

American Poetry Review: "Excalibur"
At Length: "Electric Dress"
Bennington Review: "Ixion at the Museo del Prado" and "Photograph of Thomas Edison at Mathew Brady's Studio, 1878"
BODY Literature: "Why I Have Not Written (#4)"
Colorado Review: "Nickerson Beach"
Cortland Review: "Lavender" and "Electrocuting an Elephant"
Fifth Wednesday Journal: "Crossing Tsing Ma Bridge," "Shotgun, Rabies," "Why I Have Not Written (#1, #2, #3)"
Jai-Alai: "Every Planet is a Greeting"
Massachusetts Review: "The Purity Instinct"
MiPoesias: "Invocation to Electricity"
Missouri Review: "Cassini"
New England Review: "Septimania"
Quiddity: "Illuminated"
Poetry: "Psychomachia," "Equator Sky, Manila Bay"
River Styx: "A Thousand Flowers"
Spoon River Poetry Review: "Electrolux"
Waxwing: "Poolside"

"The Face" appeared in the catalog for *Pursuing the Ephemeral, Painting the Enduring: Alzheimer's and the Artwork of William Utermohlen*, Illinois Wesleyan University, 2015.

"A Thousand Flowers" appeared in *Wherever I'm At: An Anthology of Chicago Poetry*, edited by Donald G. Evans and Robin Metz. After Hours Press, 2022.

"Septimania" appeared in *New Poetry of the Midwest*, edited by Hannah Stephenson and Rita Mae Reese. New American Press, 2021.

Thanks to the Virginia Center for the Creative Arts, the Ragdale Foundation, the Kimmel Harding Nelson Center, the Sustainable Arts Foundation, and Illinois Wesleyan University for supporting this work. I am indebted, too, to my most thoughtful readers and friends, many of whom inspired these poems through workshops, prompts, revision sessions, and writing dates: Bob Broad, Katy Didden, Jonathan Farmer, Carmela Ferradáns, Gabriel Fried, Danielle Legros Georges, Steve Halle, Ann Hudson, Jane Lin, Carolyn Nadeau, Angela Sorby, Bianca Stone, Grace Talusan, Michael Theune, Abram Van Engen, and Laura Van Prooyen. Special thanks to Peter Covino, Sharon Dolin, Rachel Rothenberg, and Charles Kell of Barrow Street Press for selecting this book for publication and sharing their keen editorial insights. And, as always, thanks to Jason Reblando, who has taught me everything I know about how to look and truly see, and to our son August, who was my most excellent companion on many of the walks that led to these poems.

Photo by Jason Reblando

Joanne Diaz is the author of *The Lessons* (winner of the Gerald Cable First Book Award from Silverfish Review Press) and *My Favorite Tyrants* (winner of the Brittingham Award from the University of Wisconsin Press). With Ian Morris, she is the co-editor of *The Little Magazine in Contemporary America* (University of Chicago Press), and she is the co-host, with Abram Van Engen, of the *Poetry for All* podcast. She is the recipient of fellowships from the Illinois Arts Council and the National Endowment for the Arts, and she has also received fellowships from Ragdale and the Virginia Center for Creative Arts. She is the Isaac Funk Professor of English at Illinois Wesleyan University.

BARROW STREET PRESS — recent titles:

Electric Dress Joanne Diaz 2026
ZOUNDS! Aleksander Zywicki 2025
Unlikely Skylight, Hollis Kurman 2025
Secret Agent Man, Margot Singer 2025
An Anthology of Rain, Phillis Levin 2025
Spare, Michelle Lewis 2025
The Mouth Is Also a Compass, Carrie Bennett 2024
Brutal Companion, Ruben Quesada 2024
Brother Nervosa, Ronald Palmer 2024
The Fire Road, Nicholas Yingling 2024
Close Red Water, Emma Aylor 2023
Fanling in October, Pui Ying Wong 2023
Landscape with Missing River, Joni Wallace 2023
Down Low and Lowdown..., Timothy Liu 2023
the archive is all in present tense, Elizabeth Hoover 2022
Person, Perceived Girl, A.A. Vincent 2022
Frank Dark, Stephen Massimilla 2022
Liar, Jessica Cuello 2021
On the Verge of Something Bright and Good, Derek Pollard 2021
The Little Book of No Consolation, Becka Mara McKay 2021
Shoreditch, Miguel Murphy 2021
Hey Y'all Watch This, Chris Hayes 2020
Uses of My Body, Simone Savannah 2020
Vortex Street, Page Hill Starzinger 2020
Exorcism Lessons in the Heartland, Cara Dees 2019
American Selfie, Curtis Bauer 2019
Hold Sway, Sally Ball 2019
Green Target, Tina Barr 2018
Luminous Debris: New & Selected Legerdemain, Timothy Liu 2018
We Step into the Sea: New and Selected Poems, Claudia Keelan 2018
Adorable Airport, Jacqueline Lyons 2018
Whiskey, X-ray, Yankee, Dara-Lyn Shrager 2018
For a complete list of publications go to: https://barrowstreet.org